LETTING
GOD SPEAK
THROUGH YOU!

LETTING GOD SPEAK THROUGH YOU!

Tracy Williamson

New Wine Press

New Wine Ministries
PO Box 17
Chichester
West Sussex
United Kingdom
PO20 6YB

Scripture quotations are taken from the following version of the Bible:

NIV – The Holy Bible, New International Version
Copyright © 1973, 1978, 1984 by International Bible Society.
Used by permission of Hodder and Stoughton Limited.

NKJV – The Holy Bible, New King James Version
Copyright © 1982 by Thomas Nelson Inc.

NLT – The Holy Bible, New Living Translation
Copyright © 1996 by Tyndale Charitable Trust.
Used by permission of Tyndale House Publishers.

All stories in this book are true and as accurate as possible. If there are any
minor details that are incorrect it is accidental and I apologise. For the sake
of confidentiality I have not generally given peoples' names

ISBN 1-903725-49-6

Typeset by CRB Associates, Reepham, Norfolk
Cover design by CCD, www.ccdgroup.co.uk
Printed in Malta

CONTENTS

DEDICATION

I dedicate this book to all those I meet who long to hear the Lord and speak His words of love. God has chosen you and anointed you. No one can show His love in just the way you can.

ACKNOWLEDGEMENTS

Thank you Tim, for your belief in me, enabling this book to be born.

Thanks to my leaders and friends at Garston Church whose early love and trust released me to step out in the prophetic.

Thanks to the many friends whose lives and ministries have been such an inspiration and particularly to those who work and play alongside me and show me so much of Jesus.

Thanks to all those whose stories I have used, both from books and personal contacts.

Thank you Marilyn for all the support and time you have given me for the writing of this book and your trust in me over the years, enabling me to step out.

Most of all, thank You Father, Son and Holy Spirit. Without You, none of this would be!

FOREWORD

I've worked alongside Tracy for many years now and know that she cannot easily enter into conversations because of her deafness. Yet I am repeatedly awed when God gives her such accurate and encouraging insights for people. These insights can literally change their lives and they know that their wonderful Heavenly Father has not forgotten them.

Do you want to be used like that? Tracy's heart passion in this book is to show us that God can and will use all of us whose hearts are open to Him, to speak His beautiful words of life to those around us and bring fresh hope, healing and awareness of His love. Tracy helps us to avoid common pitfalls and makes Isaiah 50:4 an exciting reality for us all.

A very practical and inspiring book.

Marilyn Baker

INTRODUCTION

I am drowning. The water closes over my face and I cannot breathe. But no panic, instead an incredible peace deeper than I've ever experienced. My old life ending, a new life beginning. The water presses down on me. Silence. Death. But, I am raised up! Air, Light, Transformation, Joy.

MY BAPTISM

As I came up from the water a man began to speak. There was definiteness yet gentleness to his tone that filled me with awe. I had never heard anyone pray in quite that way before. Because I am deaf I could not hear the actual words, but it was recorded and later written down for me. It was then that I discovered that it was not actually a prayer at all, but a prophetic message from God.

"Just as I have caused you to hear in your natural ears, My daughter, so you will hear with your spiritual ears. I will speak My words of love through you to those I love and long to draw close to My heart. For I am the Lord who delights in revealing the secrets of My heart to those who love Me."

I had never come across a prophetic word before and had no concept of what it meant. That it indicated I would also be prophesying did not register with me at all. What did register was the fact that the first part of it was wrong! The church leaders had prayed for my hearing to be restored as I went down into the water. They then tested it by whispering "Jesus" in my ear! The church was silent and hearing the "J" sound I guessed it would be Jesus. When I said His name the whole church erupted into cheers! I was swept up in the euphoria, but I knew deep down that while everything else in me felt fresh and new, my hearing had not actually changed.

Because that part was inaccurate I presumed all of it was, so I shelved it!

At that stage I had many areas of emotional pain and struggle in my life. I had been a Christian for only a few weeks and was also having to face the fact that my deafness was making it very difficult to complete my teaching degree. I transferred to a BA degree but felt alienated from the others who had been together on the course for a year. It was impossible to think of God speaking through me in the way the word had expressed. How could He use someone with so many problems?

The wonder of God is that when He speaks something that is from His heart, He brings it to pass. I forgot the word, but He didn't. He began to bring it about by showing me how He does it! Over the next few months He caused others to reach out to me with words and actions that shone His light and love into my own life. Paul begins his second letter to the Corinthians with a wonderful praise statement of how God works in this way in our lives:

"Praise be to the God and Father of our Lord Jesus Christ, the Father of compassion and the God of all comfort, who comforts us in all our troubles, so that we can comfort those in any trouble with the comfort we ourselves have received from God."

(2 Corinthians 1:3–4)

We cannot give out of nothing! The intention of God in giving us gifts of communication is to build up, edify and comfort those we share them with. But we all have, to some degree, an inner "hole" that is filled with the pains, regrets, stresses and fears of a lifetime. These in turn often fuel negative life motivators of anger, hopelessness, bitterness, or fear. Learning to receive the ongoing, personal compassion and comfort of our Father God means that hole is transformed into a well of compassion, from which we can share God's words of love for others. We cannot receive God's comfort and compassion without developing "hearing" ears to His voice. God will speak to us in many ways, all of which can build us up and transform us from within and also equip us to share His supernatural gifts of communication with others

The Start of the Word's Fulfilment

Some two years after I received that prophecy at my baptism I went to my first event with the blind singer, Marilyn Baker. I thought I was just helping her out until she found a new assistant and had no idea that God was preparing me to join her ministry! I had actually completely forgotten the prophecy but God was doing a deep healing and releasing work in my life, and in that process I'd experienced hearing His voice.

As Marilyn and I were preparing for the evening service, she said to me: "Can you listen to see if the Lord gives you any thoughts from His heart to share tonight?" I said, "yes", without having a clue what she meant! But I tried to still my heart and to reach out to God, asking Him if there was anything He wanted to show me. To my amazement ideas began to pop into my mind. They were just simple little thoughts to do with God wanting to comfort someone feeling very lonely, someone else recently bereaved etc. I later shared them in the service and at the end we were able to pray with several who came forward in response. Many also became Christians and rededicated their lives to God. Marilyn and I were filled with awe at what God had done. It made us understand in a new way His incredible love and long for more of His power to communicate effectively. It made me remember my baptism prophecy and to pray that God would make it real in my life.

I am still praying that prayer now! There are always new things to discover and explore in the adventure of letting God speak through *me*.

Do you want to join me on this adventure? Then read on! But please do more than just read! Take it in. Try the exercises and ideas. Pray. Receive. And then step out into the joy of learning to share what He gives you.

Tracy Williamson

CHAPTER 1

DO YOU KNOW THE HOLY SPIRIT?

*"You will receive power when the Holy Spirit comes on you;
and you will be my witnesses . . ."*
(ACTS 1:8)

Some months after I became a Christian I went to a celebration worship event. The worship was exuberant, with many raising hands, dancing and shouting out their praises to God. Suddenly, a lady turned to me and said,

"Aren't you baptised in the Holy Spirit?"

Somewhat surprised I replied, "Yes, I am."

She looked at me doubtfully, obviously not convinced. "Well, why aren't you dancing like everyone else then?"

This conversation shows the misunderstanding many have about the Holy Spirit. The Holy Spirit is not an experience, a powerful force or a charismatic way of worshipping. He is a Person, the very Person of God. He fills our lives with the transforming power of Jesus' death and resurrection. The joy and love we then experience, release us to worship God with abandon. However, that abandonment is a *result* of what the Bible calls *"being baptised in the Holy Spirit"*. The baptism itself means that we have stepped through a doorway into a new depth and reality of relationship with God. It is the beginning of an adventure of hearing God's voice, speaking His words and doing His works, all in the power of His love. In that celebration meeting I was not "bopping" like everyone else because with my poor balance I find it difficult! I don't have to be bopping to prove I am filled with the Holy Spirit. The proof is within me, in His gifts and fruit manifested in my life, in my deeper love for God and in my desire to make Him known.

When I asked Jesus to baptise me with His Holy Spirit, I didn't understand all that I was asking for. Do we ever? I was attending a charismatic Christian Fellowship and had seen people praying in tongues, prophesying, being delivered and engaging in very free worship. I presumed that if God answered my prayer, I would be taken over by an all-encompassing force that would make me say and do strange things! I was pretty scared of this happening as control had always been my defence mechanism and I didn't want to lose that or to look weird! But deeper than that fear was another: I was afraid that nothing would happen at all and I was desperate for God to work in my life.

I was wrong on both counts!

At first I felt nothing at all! It seemed that my deepest fear had been realised – God had left me out and I went to bed depressed. The next day I walked from my college hostel to the main campus. The route passed through a scenic golf course which I had walked countless times and hardly seen! I started in my usual distracted mode, but suddenly stopped. I gazed around, noticing as if for the first time the beauty and peace. I couldn't stop drinking it in. I was alone and yet I had the strangest feeling that someone was standing next to me. In the stillness I had a clear impression of words coming into my consciousness. "I made all this for you to enjoy, for you to see how much I love you."

Awestruck I realised that this was God. I had never heard His voice speaking so clearly and full of friendship. All the way it was as if He was pointing different things out to me, just like a friend. Everything seemed so beautiful, as if it had been painted in bright new colours. Similarly, in the seminars. Because of my deafness, I had always found the seminars a battle and often felt humiliated by my inability to respond intelligently. This day, I went in feeling much more peaceful, but with no expectation that anything would be any different. I was amazed when thoughts came into my mind just at the moment the lecturer asked me for my contribution! I shared, not even knowing what they'd been discussing! The lecturer said, "Thank you Tracy, that was very illuminating, I've never heard that perspective on this subject before!" I was staggered to think that God could inspire my thinking in educational philosophy and psychology. I thought He was only interested in "religious" things!

God had spoken into my spirit His own deep thoughts and helped me like a friend. This filled me joy and awe as I realised that God had truly answered my prayer. I had met with Someone who communicated powerfully enough to free me from self preoccupation and fear but gently enough that I was still completely "Trace" with all my quirks and foibles. I was excited and expectant that I was embarking on an adventure with the Holy Spirit as my friend. Later I found this passage in 1 Corinthians which brought alive to me what had been happening that day:

> " 'No eye has seen,
>   no ear has heard,
>   no mind has conceived
>   what God has prepared for those who love Him' –

> but God has revealed it to us by his Spirit. The spirit searches all things, even the deep things of God. For who among men knows the thoughts of a man except the man's spirit within him? In the same way no-one knows the thoughts of God except the Spirit of God. We have not received the spirit of the world but the Spirit who is from God, that we may understand what God has freely given us . . .

> 'For who has known the mind of the Lord
>   that he may instruct Him?'

> But we have the mind of Christ."

(1 CORINTHIANS 2:9–12, 16)

Love Means Communication

Many of us do not realise that it is the essence of God's character to communicate. We go through our Christian lives diligently serving Him, yet never developing real, intimate relationship with Him. Yet Jesus showed that our effectiveness as Christians depends on this very thing:

> *"I no longer call you servants, because a servant does not know his master's business. Instead, I have called you friends, for everything that I learned from my Father I have made known to you. You did not choose me, but I chose you ... to go and bear fruit — fruit that will last."*
>
> (JOHN 15:15–16)

In my book, *Expecting God to Speak to You!* I explore the wonder of the fact that God our Father loves to communicate with us. He wants to draw close and build us up in His love, to minister healing and strength into our inner beings, to guide us and empower us. I discovered early in my Christian life that there were no limits to how He might communicate. The key is to be open to the Holy Spirit, who is, if you like, the mouth of God. As that verse in 1 Corinthians 2 expresses, He is the One who knows the very heart and thoughts of God, because He *is* the heart and thoughts of God. Jesus Himself was only able to do and say the things He did because of His dependence on the Holy Spirit. The Spirit came to Jesus at His baptism and Jesus heard God say:

> *"This is my Son, whom I love; with him I am well pleased."*
>
> (MATTHEW 3:17)

Through the Spirit, Jesus' heart was opened in this new way to the affirming words of God. He would need these, as we all do, to root Him in the truth of who He was and what He was to be as the Son of God. The Spirit also opened His eyes, giving Him ongoing revelation to see and hear what the Father was doing. Thus Jesus was given such a mission blueprint that He was able to say:

"I tell you the truth, the Son can do nothing by himself; he can do only what he sees his Father doing, because whatever the Father does the Son also does. For the Father loves the Son and shows him all he does."

(JOHN 5:19–20)

REVELATION RELEASES THE POWER OF GOD

Jesus spoke the above words about His relationship with the Father immediately after healing a man who had been crippled for thirty-eight years. It was no mere chance that Jesus engaged this particular man in conversation. They were at the pool of Bethesda, a place where countless sick people gathered in the desperate hope of healing. This man was just one of many, but I believe that as Jesus saw the mass of needs, the Holy Spirit drew that particular man to His attention, so much so that Jesus felt compelled to make enquiries about him. He learned that the man had suffered from his crippling condition for a very long time. As Jesus listened to the information He also listened to the Holy Spirit and knew that this was someone that His Heavenly Father wanted to heal. Jesus also discerned that his affliction was the result of sin in the man's life. With the wisdom of the Holy Spirit's guidance, He then spoke with the man encouraging him to tell his story and listening with respect. Then with the power and confidence that could only come from a heart in tune with God's will, He commanded the man to get up and walk and he did! Jesus left him to enjoy his healing, but did not forget the revelation about his sinful lifestyle. Later, He found the man again and said to him. *"See, you are well again. Stop sinning or something worse may happen to you"* (John 5:14; whole story 1–16). I believe these words came with prophetic power into the man's heart and enabled him not just be healed but to change his whole lifestyle.

WE CAN EXPERIENCE THIS POWER TO CHANGE LIVES TOO!

Not long after praying to be filled with the Holy Spirit, I was on a young people's weekend. One of the leaders prophesied that someone needed to stop running and commit themselves to God. No one responded and after a while the meeting ended.

As I went upstairs I prayed quietly that the right person would be able to respond. A girl passed me and suddenly I sensed a voice inside me saying, "This is the person." I was shocked! Was I just imagining things? Then another thought came to me.

"Tell her that she needs to let go of her boyfriend because he won't give her the happiness she is looking for and is standing in the way of her coming to Me!"

By now I was shaking! I couldn't possibly say that to her!

"Lord, I can hardly remember what she looked like and I don't even know her name!"

Just then someone came round the corner and with disbelief I recognised the girl!

"Can I have a word?" I asked diffidently.

"Yes, what is it?"

"Well, I felt God might be saying that the prophecy in the meeting was for you." I paused but she didn't say anything, so I blundered on. "He seemed to say that you need to give your boyfriend up because he is stopping you finding the happiness that only God can give you!"

There it was out! I looked down at the floor expecting a torrent of angry words and was startled when she said quietly, "Can we talk?"

We talked for two hours then went to bed. The following evening I was full of joy when I saw her go forward at the end of the meeting to become a Christian." [1]

THE POWERFUL EFFECT OF GOD'S WORDS

Because of the impact upon her of the voice of God, this girl became a Christian. She could have been very offended! After all, I was a complete stranger bringing up a very personal issue in her life. But she did not react that way at all. It was as if what was said opened up an awareness of her own need. Rather than taking offence, she realised that God knew and loved her. This gave her the impetus to respond to Him.

As Paul says in 1 Corinthians 14:24–25 (précis),

"If an unbeliever or someone who does not understand comes in while everybody is prophesying ... the secrets of his heart will be laid bare ... he will fall down and worship God, exclaiming, 'God is really among you!'"

It wasn't that it was a mystical experience; the prophecy in the meeting was very down to earth. No one responded and the girl went her way with everyone else. But something must have been happening in her heart. God knew this. He loved her and would not give up until He had reached her, so He spoke to me in that specific way. What I received from Him was a combination of what the Bible calls a word of knowledge and a prophetic message. A word of knowledge is divinely inspired knowledge about a person or situation that we could never know ourselves. Like Jesus identifying the man in the crowd at Bethesda, there was no way among two hundred or so young people that I could know this girl's needs, or that she wasn't a Christian, I thought they all were! I certainly wouldn't have known anything about her boyfriend! The prophetic message revealed God's understanding and love. He wasn't speaking as a tyrant telling her she couldn't have boyfriends, but as a loving Father seeing the effect on her life her boyfriend would have and wanting to lead her into a truer place of fulfilment. As with the man at Bethesda receiving healing as Jesus spoke under the inspiration of the Holy Spirit, so this girl was able to start on a new journey because of the powerful effect on her of God's words.

WILL YOU LET GOD SPEAK THROUGH YOU?

As I wrote this section I was listening to one of Marilyn's songs called "When I Think". The final verse (based on 1 Corinthians 2:9–16) says:

"Who can know the mind of the Lord,
Or who can know what He is thinking?
And yet we have the mind of Christ,
So we can know His thoughts deep within us
And be part of what He is doing." [2]

I don't know about you, but I long with all my heart to be part of what God is doing. I am so weak, but then so were the disciples! They were full of wrong motivations, misunderstandings about Jesus' mission and petty rivalries. They were, in the main, uneducated and naïve. They had little faith and were often full of fear and inadequacy. In fact, you could apply this as a character description of all God's followers since creation! Out of fear Abram pretended Sarai was only his sister. Moses committed murder, hid in the desert and when commissioned by God tried to use his stammer as an excuse not to act. Elijah also fled to the desert. Jeremiah felt inadequate because of his youth. David committed adultery and arranged a murder. Gideon was fearful. Jonah tried to run away and was full of self-pity. Jacob was a cheat. Paul was a persecutor of the Church...!

Yet, they all communicated God's voice so powerfully that their society was totally changed!

The fact is that if God had only ever wanted to use perfect people there would have been no story of His dealings with mankind! It is not perfect people that He calls, but you and me! And then, as we respond, He says with love:

"I know you are not perfect, but I am! And I see you covered with the perfection of My Son. Because of Him your weaknesses

are blotted out and I give you the gift of His inner strength. I am perfect in My commitment to you. I will never leave you without support or forsake you in any way. I give you the perfect gifts of My Spirit's love, resources and power. You can do all things with Me alongside you and within you. Only let Me be there. Open up to Me and let Me open up to you and reveal My heart to you. Trust in Me and see what I can do through you." [3]

Maybe you'd like to pray this prayer with me?

"Thank You Lord Jesus for the priceless gift of Your love. Thank You that You call me to know You and be part of what You are doing. Lord I feel so weak, but You promise me Your very own Spirit that I might have all the spiritual resources I need. Lord I want this wonderful gift. Please fill me Holy Spirit and open my eyes to see God, my ears to hear His voice, and my heart to love and obey Him. Thank You that You have heard and answered this prayer. Amen."

CHAPTER 2

RECEIVING LIKE LITTLE CHILDREN

"... anyone who comes to him must believe ...
that he rewards those who earnestly seek him."
(HEBREWS 11:6)

ASKING AND RECEIVING

Recently I met a lady and while chatting with her, I prayed quietly that God would show me if there was any particular way He wanted to bless her. The thought came that she was lonely and felt she couldn't make good relationships. I sensed God was saying that He had made her to be a joy and delight to people and He was going to establish her in good relationships where she could give as well as receive. I shared this with her, asking her if it rang true in any way? She told me that she had recently moved to a new area and was finding it very difficult to build up relationships again. She was very encouraged by this prophetic word. She left with a new sense of hope and joy that God truly knew and was with her.

THE JOY OF GOD SPEAKING THROUGH US

That lady was encouraged, but so was I! There is something very wonderful about knowing that you have brought divinely inspired encouragement or challenge to someone. It is not the joy of being right so much as the joy of knowing that you are in partnership with God. That you and He are working together on something so incredibly worthwhile. It is the joy of being privy to His deep thoughts and desires to reach out with His love. It is the joy of seeing someone lifted up, blessed and touched by the Spirit of God.

WHO AM I TO ASK?

You may notice that I said that I asked God specifically to reveal to me if there was any way He wanted to bless the lady. Do you think that is a presumptuous prayer to pray? Who am I to think that I will hear what God wants to say to someone else? It's OK if God initiates it, but who am I to ask for it to happen?

There is a wonderful verse in Hebrews that addresses this very issue:

"Let us then approach the throne of grace with confidence, so that we may receive mercy and find grace to help us in our time of need."

(HEBREWS 4:16)

Many of us think of grace as simply being God's undeserved favour. It is that of course, but the word "favour" signifies a huge amount. It means "the fullness of God's resources, love, mercy, divine gifts and power". Because of that undeserved favour, Jesus is now within us and everywhere we go we reveal what God is like. How exciting to think that we are part of God's strategy to establish His Kingdom of love and mercy in our dark world. But God also wants to make His Kingdom known in specific ways and to specific people or situations. For that to happen He needs to brief us with specific understanding. Without any fear of being presumptuous we can come to Him and say, "Here I am Lord. What do You want to tell me?"

BUT HOW DOES THIS HAPPEN?

In the last chapter we thought about how we can know the Holy Spirit. Jesus said to His disciples,

"You will receive power when the Holy Spirit comes on you; and you will be my witnesses..."

(ACTS 1:8)

As Jesus makes clear, for us to truly be His witnesses, we need the anointing of the Holy Spirit. He is the only one who knows the mind and heart of God. His ministry then, is to reveal that mind and heart to us, as Jesus expressed, *"He will take of what is Mine and declare it to you"* (John 16:14 NKJV). As a deaf person I find that an amazing thought. Humanly, I struggle when I miss out on what people are saying. It is especially difficult if everyone is deeply involved in some conversation which I can't follow. Wonderfully though, I have many caring friends who help me know what is going on. They say this is a joy. Conversely, they feel sad if they know that I am not getting things. That is humbling and makes me very thankful, but it is incredible to think that the Holy Spirit fulfils that very same role with us. It is God's passionate desire that we know what is going on in the heavenly realms and are filled with His own power and resources to do His works.

> **Do you believe God wants to give *you* the anointing and resources to do His works?**

An Exercise

Before reading further, spend a few moments with God. Acknowledge in your heart that He loves you and wants to bless you.

Now read Mark 1:40–42:

"A man with leprosy came to [Jesus] *and begged him on his knees, 'If you are willing, you can make me clean.'*

Filled with compassion, Jesus reached out his hand and touched the man. 'I am willing,' he said. 'Be clean!' Immediately the leprosy left him and he was cured."

The key to us receiving the Holy Spirit's power to speak and do His works is in us understanding not only what God can *do*, but what He is *like*.

This man knew what Jesus *could* do, that He had the power to heal, but he didn't know what Jesus *would* do. He was not sure if Jesus would want to help him.

Are you in the same position?

Think about this story and ask yourself the following questions. You may like to jot down your answers.

1. Do I identify with the leper in any way? If so how?
2. Do I expect Jesus to respond to me, or do I feel that I am not important enough?
3. Despite the leper's fear that Jesus would be unwilling to help, he still came and asked, in fact, he begged. Do I still come to Jesus, despite any fears I may have about His willingness? Am I honest with Him as the leper was about my fears?
4. What does Jesus' response to the leper say to me?
5. Jesus' compassion and love freed this man from the grip of terrible disease. Will I choose to believe He loves me and wants to give me all that I need?

Spend some time talking to God about your responses. If you realised that you do not have much expectancy for Him to respond to you, pray He will open your mind and heart to know Him better. You may like to use the prayer that Paul prayed for the Ephesians:

"I keep asking that the God of our Lord Jesus Christ, the glorious Father, may give you the Spirit of wisdom and revelation, so that you may know him better ... And I pray that you, being rooted and established in love, may have power ... to grasp how wide and long and high and deep is the love of Christ, and to know this love that surpasses knowledge – that you may be filled to the measure of all the fullness of God."

(EPHESIANS 1:17; 3:17–19)

EXPECTING TO RECEIVE

I once had a friend come to stay with her little girl of four, Sarah. Sarah had never met Marilyn or me. I thought that would make her shy and so she was – at first! But that shyness did not last long. We went shopping and in no time Sarah was full of excited expectancy that the sole reason for their visit was for her to receive! Whether it was a cuddle, a drink, a sweet or a new toy, she knew what she needed and asked for it without hesitation! She received much of what she asked for, but by no means everything! But even when the answer was a firm "NO" it never deterred her from asking again, and again and again!

Sarah, as all children, had an unshaken belief in her right to be given to and therefore to receive. Unless a child has come from a very deprived or cruel home they expect to be provided for as a matter of course. Obviously, children must learn that they cannot have everything they ask for. As they get older they also learn what things are appropriate to ask for and when. Older still, they may learn another, but untrue lesson – that they should not ask for personal things at all! This often comes under the heading of "Being

Christlike". Many adults in our churches today feel it is vaguely sinful to express personal needs and desires, either to people or to God.

Although this attitude seems sacrificial and spiritual, it is not actually biblical! The theme of confidently asking and receiving comes up again and again throughout the New Testament and is one of the key elements of Jesus' teaching.

> *"Ask and it will be given to you; seek and you will find; knock and the door will be opened to you. For everyone who asks receives; he who seeks finds; and to him who knocks, the door will be opened. Which of you, if his son asks for bread, will give him a stone? Or if he asks for a fish, will give him a snake? If you then, though you are evil, know how to give good gifts to your children, how much more will your Father in heaven give good gifts to those who ask him!"*
>
> (MATTHEW 7:7–11)

The issue of asking and receiving was so important to Jesus that He repeated it six times and then rounded it off with a graphic illustration from everyday life. Six times Jesus says: Your Heavenly Daddy loves to give to you. Your Heavenly Daddy loves to answer you. Your Heavenly Daddy is watching and listening and full of eagerness to respond to you.

It is vital that we understand this because it is one of the main keys to us learning to let God speak through us. The following story demonstrates how effective we can be when we come to Him with an expectation that He wants to help and equip us.

A Wonderful Healing

When Marilyn was in her late twenties she had constant crippling stomach pains. She'd had them for as long as she could remember but the doctors dismissed it as "migraine of the stomach". She was a teacher and each day was a struggle to get through. One day she went to visit a friend who immediately commented on how ill Marilyn looked. Marilyn told her why and the friend said, "Have you prayed about it?"

"I'm sick of praying," Marilyn responded. "I've prayed till I'm blue in the face and nothing ever changes!"

"But have you ever asked God to show you the root?" her friend persisted.

Marilyn was not sure, so agreed to let her pray. To Marilyn's surprise her friend did not launch into pleas for healing as others had done, but quietly and simply asked God to reveal if there was any root to the illness. Then she waited.

"Were you in an oxygen tent as a baby?" she asked after a few minutes silence.

Shocked, Marilyn said that yes, she was, because of being premature.

"Well," her friend said, "I had this impression come to my mind of you in there as a tiny baby, feeling very alone and afraid and wanting your mum. Will you let me pray that God will come into that memory and take away your fear and give you His security and comfort?"

Rather uncertainly Marilyn agreed. During the prayer she just felt a slight sense of peace, but she was still in pain. The next day she went to work as usual. Back home, she was cooking her tea when she suddenly realised she had no pain! The next day, again, no pain. She's never had one since!

Later, as Marilyn reflected, she realised that the pains had started when she was sent to boarding school at five years old, but she never had them in the school holidays. The enforced separation of school had set off those buried memories from her birth experience. It was a physical condition with an emotional root – a root only God could have known about. Hearing what that root was led to this wonderful healing.

Hearing God – the Key to Letting Him Speak Through Us

Marilyn had been pleading with God to heal her for years. Many friends were also praying for her. Yet her condition had just got worse. This is always very discouraging and often makes us feel there's no point in praying. The fact is, God alone knows the full picture and can see the hidden things that we are not aware of. To take time to listen as well as to plead is the key to effective prayer. As we listen He will then be able to reveal to us any root to the problem or any way He particularly wants to work.

The friend in this story did not plead with God. Instead she asked Him to speak to her. She had a calm expectancy that God *would* speak. She wanted Him to, because she knew that if God revealed a key then she would be able to pray for Marilyn with a certainty about what He wanted to do. Her prayer for Him to speak was expectant and relaxed. She believed in her own right as His child ministering in His name, to hear His heart for the situation.

Jesus showed this same assurance in the way He talked to God at the moment of raising Lazarus from the dead:

"Father, I thank you that you have heard me. I knew that you always hear me, but I said this for the benefit of the people standing here, that they may believe that you sent me."

(JOHN 11:41–42)

Jesus had confidence that God heard and responded to His prayers. Marilyn's friend had confidence that she would hear God. These are two sides of the same coin. Prayer is not a case of finding the right words and hopefully hitting the bull's-eye. It is all to do with relationship – having a heart certainty about the character of the One you are praying to and of your right to hear and receive from Him because of being His beloved child. Because Jesus had nurtured in His Spirit the fact that God was His Father, He was able to *tune in* to what God wanted Him to do and *tune out* all the panicky voices of those around Him.

A PRAYER

"Lord God, thank You that it is Your joy to 'graciously give us all things'. Forgive me Lord that I've never had the faith to ask You for what I need. Forgive me too that I've had such a small understanding of what You are like. Please make me like a little child running to You my 'Abba' with that joyful expectation that You are listening and responding. Thank You Father. Amen."

AN IMAGINATIVE EXERCISE

1. Think of a person or situation where you would love to see God working. In prayer lift them/it up to God and ask Him what is needed to bring His blessing and help. Jot down any thoughts that come.

2. Now: Imagine you are Marilyn and cannot see. She has a guest coming and wants to cook a nice meal. She decides what she needs and goes to the shop. But Marilyn obviously can't serve herself. She has to ask the shopkeeper to find the items for her. In the same way, as we've listened to God we have an idea of what we need, but we can't find it in ourselves. We need to ask our Heavenly Shopkeeper for it.

3. Shut your eyes and imagine stepping blindly into the Kingdom Resources Shop. Hear the Shopkeeper saying, "Hello there, how can I help you?"

4. Tell Him each item you need.

5. Take the full carrier bag. Thank the Shopkeeper and leave.

6. Go home and cook your meal! (or in other words – take what you have just received and apply it to the situation you've been praying about.)

CHAPTER 3

HOW DOES
GOD SPEAK
THROUGH US?

"The Sovereign LORD has given me an instructed tongue
to know the word that sustains the weary.
He wakens me morning by morning,
wakens my ear to listen like one being taught.
The Sovereign LORD has opened my ears,
and I have not been rebellious;
I have not drawn back."
(ISAIAH 50:4–5)

UNDERSTAND THE "WHY" BEFORE LOOKING AT THE "HOW"!

A lady in a deep depression came to a conference. She believed she had made so many wrong lifestyle choices that she had lost the Lord. She felt such a failure, but her very condemnation was stopping her from receiving the Lord's forgiveness.

One evening during the worship, I glanced at a picture of a vine on the wall. One of its branches had fallen off and was withering on the ground. I couldn't take my mind off that branch so asked God if He was speaking to me. He answered, "Someone here feels like that branch. They have been sitting here staring at that very picture thinking 'I am that branch, I don't belong to God like the others do. I am separate and all the fruit He has looked for in me is withering.' But that is a lie. They are only that branch in their condemned imagination. In reality they are like that topmost branch in the picture. They are My number one and I have grafted them into My heart. Nothing can ever remove them from that place of My love."

I shared this word and later that lady responded. The first thing she said was: "I knew God was speaking to me through you. I'd been sitting in my seat staring at that very picture thinking, 'I am that branch that has fallen off.' I couldn't believe it when you said that very thing. Please can you pray for me?" By the end of the conference that dear lady knew without any doubt that she was completely reconciled to God. She'd arrived in the pits, she left dancing!

On another occasion a friend, Lilian, shared a prophetic picture of an infant holding onto a chair. The Lord was standing a short distance away, encouraging the child to let go of the chair and walk towards Him. The interpretation was that God had called someone to do something for Him but they were holding back because of fear. Another team member later responded and took the word to heart asking Lilian to intercede for her when later she had to minister to a disabled lady. Because of this word, she ministered with a new confidence and authority and the lady was wonderfully healed of the effects of a stroke.

These stories speak so much of the "why" we need to let God speak though us, as well as the "how". Many vital things are taught about God but on their own are not always enough to set free, heal and empower. God also wants to speak directly and specifically to people. For that to happen there needs to be someone willing to listen and pass on God's message as He directs. Such a message from God cuts like a sword to the heart of the issue because it comes from the Holy Spirit. It comforts, convicts and creates life and peace because these are all His ministries.

God longs to reach out and transform peoples lives, for them to know Him and become like Jesus. He longs for those who are broken by life to be healed and in partnership with Him to build His Church that, *"... the gates of hell will not overcome it"* (Matthew 16:18).

Letting God speak through us is never to do with words that we speak mindlessly like robots. We are bombarded with enough of that in the media! It is our lives, characters and attitudes as much as anything we say. It is our willingness to submit our own judgements to God and receive His divine understanding and knowledge in whatever way He wants to give it us.

THERE ARE FIVE PRIMARY WAYS THAT GOD WANTS TO SPEAK THROUGH US

1. *Through our words* – counsel, encouragement, affirmation, challenge, preaching/teaching, personal sharing/testimony.
2. *Through the gifts of the Holy Spirit* – prophecy, dreams and visions, words of knowledge, healing, discernment of spirits, tongues and interpretation.
3. *Through our prayers and intercessions.*
4. *Through our attitudes and actions* – love, hugs and smiles, forgiving hearts, kindnesses, hospitality, worship, thankfulness, peacemaking, refusal to gossip, giving.
5. *Through our creative gifts* – music, dance, art and craft, writing, cooking, homemaking, drama, childrearing, relationship building.

This is an extreme shortlist! But I hope it gives you a picture of the vastness of the ways by which God wants to speak through you! We can think in a very compartmentalised way that only the supernatural gifts like prophecy truly convey God's voice and need the Spirit's anointing, but *all these areas* need anointing and can be powerful channels for God to speak through. For example, hospitality. in Acts 6:2–6, specific disciples were set aside and anointed solely for the task of waiting on tables. It wasn't in any way considered to be of secondary importance but was essential.

One of the key ways God spoke to me when I first became a Christian was through the hospitality of a couple in my church, John and Amanda. They welcomed me into their family even for times like Christmas and holidays. Yet this was at a time when I was very needy emotionally and not always easy to have around. Their giving love spoke volumes of the reality of God's love and set me well on the road to healing.

Similarly our creative gifts need anointing and are wonderful channels of His voice. We can sometimes rank them as inferior to direct communicative gifts like preaching or prophesying, but this is not how God views them. We see in Exodus 35:31–35 how Moses recognised the Spirit's anointing upon Bezalel and others to create the tabernacle, the design of which would be constantly speaking of the glory of God.

Marilyn often doesn't know what to say when faced with a situation, yet her songs are full of the tenderness and wise counsel of the Lord. Many have been healed of grief, low self-esteem and even alcoholism through her songs, yet Marilyn was told at music college that her compositions were boring! Primarily an oboist, she gave her natural musicianship to the Lord and asked the Holy Spirit to anoint her. It was the "boring" song writing that the Lord took and transformed into a powerful channel for His voice! One of her most famous prophetic songs, *Rest In My Love*, came when she was agitated with a difficult bus journey. Suddenly the words: *"Rest in My love, relax in My care, and know that My presence will always be there. You are My child and I care for you, there's nothing My love and My power cannot do"*,[4] came to her mind. The Lord was encouraging her to let go of her anxiety because He loved her and was in control. She did relax and later, to her amazement, she found the words fitted exactly into a very peaceful tune she had recently composed. This song is now over twenty years old and has had a tremendous healing impact on people who are seriously ill or facing bereavement and life change.

Other friends who have been through terrible childhood experiences have developed creative gifts that speak to many of the love of God. One friend takes beautiful photographs then adds incredible Bible verses that give the pictures a "voice". She also makes clay pictures showing the Father love of God. She gave one to a lady once in obedience to a prompting from the Holy Spirit. She didn't say anything but it had tremendous prophetic impact on the lady who desperately needed to see the tenderness of God at that time. Another friend had a mental breakdown because of awful experiences in the Gulf War. She felt clumsy and awkward but started to express herself through worship with banners. As they have watched her many have been spoken to of God's beauty and inspired to worship creatively themselves.

One of the primary ways we speak to others is in the way we allow the Lord to love and forgive through us. Our world is so full of anger and bitterness. When someone is confronted by a Christian who has been badly hurt yet is willing to forgive and love, there is no counting the impact. Many of our prayer team have experienced abuse, rejection, physical suffering, yet their warmth, forgiving hearts and desire to love with the love of Jesus is incredibly powerful. Also, our attitudes can speak so much. We met a lady born with cerebral palsy who subsequently became further disabled by a spinal injury following a fall. Rather than becoming bitter, she began to talk to God and He told her to set herself positive goals of achievement. One was to do a walk for charity, which incredibly she achieved. Next was a public waltz with a celebrity! She also went to New York and despite becoming seriously unwell, persisted in seeing Jesus in all those who cared for and helped her during her time there. She returned full of joy. Her email starts, "Reach for the skies..." and everyone who hears her story is challenged by God to do just that.

What About the Supernatural Gifts?

Paul tells us:

> *"There are different kinds of gifts, but the same Spirit. There are different kinds of service, but the same Lord. There are different kinds of working, but the same God works all of them in all men. Now to each one the manifestation of the Spirit is given for the common good. To one there is given through the Spirit the message of wisdom, to another the message of knowledge by means of the same Spirit, to another faith ... to another gifts of healing ... to another miraculous powers, to another prophecy ... distinguishing between spirits ... speaking in different kinds of tongues, and ... the interpretation of tongues."*
>
> (1 Corinthians 12:4–10)

This is not an exhaustive list of the gifts. Paul is merely stating that God will anoint each person individually with His power and that anointing will take different forms which all harmonise together to build up the Church, reach the lost and reveal the glory of God. The gifts are not something that take us over and make us clones of one another. Instead they fit us and our unique way of being. We cannot work them up or get them by copying anyone else.

All the gifts are to do with communicating God's grace and power in various ways and although we can only receive them from God, they do often fit our "bent". Someone who is naturally intuitive and visual will be more likely to receive pictures and visions, whereas a practical, logical person may be given straightforward knowledge or a solution to a situation. Within each grouping there is also huge variation. You may have three people all gifted with wisdom, but they will all express it differently. One of them may solve people conflicts, like King Solomon with the women and baby. Another may be given the wisdom to organise events and liaise with people; yet another may have eyes to recognise and develop areas of gifting in the church.

I described in the introduction how a prophetic word was spoken over me that I would hear God's words of love for people. There were two natural areas in my life that God began to use as the "base" for this gifting. Firstly my love of reading which had developed my creative imagination, love of words and empathetic understanding of people; secondly various traumatic events of my childhood which had given me a deep awareness of the pain people can experience and a desire to help relieve it. So this intuitive, empathetic, imaginative "bent" has now become the channel through which God gives me His love words and pictures. Marilyn is also prophetically gifted and has a heart to encourage those who are struggling or broken-hearted. But never having seen physically she rarely has pictures, although when she does they are very powerful. Her primary natural gifting is musical and her personality is very loving but straightforward. Her prophetic gifting is often released in the songs she writes or in the wise way she talks with people enabling them to open up.

An Exercise

Take some time to be quiet. Have a pen and paper to hand. Ask the Lord Jesus to be with you and to speak to you by His Spirit. Slowly read these verses from Psalm 139:

"O LORD, you have examined my heart
and know everything about me.
You know when I sit down or stand up.
You know my every thought when far away . . .
Every moment you know where I am.
You know what I am going to say
even before I say it . . .
You made all the delicate, inner parts of my body
and knit me together in my mother's womb . . .
You saw me before I was born.
Every day of my life was recorded in your book.
Every moment was laid out
before a single day had passed."

(PSALM 139:1–4, 13, 16 NLT)

In the light of these words think about your life. Think about how completely known you are to God. In all your thoughts, activities, words, your inner and outer being, you are known and loved. Ask Jesus to help you see yourself as He sees you. Then ask yourself these questions:

1. What kind of things make you tick?,
2. What do you enjoy doing? Can you see qualities that have developed within you as a result?
3. Are you drawn more to words or graphics to make something clear?

4. Are you more inclined to logically judge people, situations or places by what you see, hear or know, or are you someone who feels your response and is aware of atmospheres or inner issues that aren't outwardly obvious?

5. What kind of life experiences have you had? Do you feel any deeper desire to reach out to certain people or situations because of those experiences?

6. How do you express your creativity? Don't say, "I'm not creative at all"! If you are a Christian you have the Almighty Creator of this universe living in you and you can't help but be creative! It isn't just to do with art or music or dance etc. Things like building relationships, childrearing, making a home, hosting a party, dealing with administration, all need creative input and can become powerful channels for God to speak through.

7. Spend some time reflecting over what you have written down.

8. Thank the Lord for all He's made you to be and for the way He wants to use all that you are and all you have experienced. Ask Him to bless and pour out His gifts and communicative power into each area of your life.

9. Keep what you have written in your journal. It may well become the base on which God develops His gifts within you.

"Follow the Way of Love"

In his first letter to the Corinthians Paul describes the gifts and how we are to receive and step out in them. Having already said in chapter 12 that the gifts come from the Spirit, "[who] *gives them to each one, just as he determines*" (v. 11), he then tells the Corinthians to: "*Follow the way of love and eagerly desire spiritual gifts*" (1 Corinthians 14:1).

This makes clear three important things:

1. The gifts come to us from God through the Holy Spirit. It is He who sees a need and releases the gift in order for that need to be met. It is He who determines who will be the best channel for that gift at that particular time. He is the only source, not our level of spirituality or academic qualifications etc.

2. However, Paul shows that we are not to be passively waiting for the gifts but actively seeking them. Paul says "*eagerly desire spiritual gifts*". A child at Christmas knows that his parents (or Father Christmas) will bring him presents. This does not stop him from asking for what he wants though. In fact, he asks with great enthusiasm and detail! Equally, we must ask the Holy Spirit with enthusiasm and detail. The Holy Spirit searches for those who have expectant hearts and then opens up appropriate gifts to them.

3. The key to us receiving and learning to use the gifts is the state of our hearts. Paul said specifically, "*follow the way of **love** ...*" As we perceive a need in a loved one, church or community, our hearts are touched and we ask God to enable us to bring His light and love into that need. Just getting the gifts must *never* be the point. Having the power to reach out effectively with God's love and to draw closer to God Himself must *always* be the point.

KNOWING GOD AND PERCEIVING WHAT HE WANTS TO SAY

When God told Jonah to go to Nineveh to preach against their sin and declare the Lord's judgement, he ran away! The reason he ran away was because he was afraid the Lord would not fulfil the word! "What will they think of me then?" kept running through his mind. It is so easy to have our thoughts on what people will think of us rather than seeking the Lord to know what He is really saying. Even when Jonah eventually preached the word to Nineveh he still hadn't grasped what God really wanted to do.

"The Ninevites believed God. They declared a fast, and all of them, from the greatest to the least, put on sackcloth ... When God saw what they did and how they turned from their evil ways, he had compassion and did not bring upon them the destruction he had threatened. But Jonah was greatly displeased and became angry."

(JONAH 3:5, 10; 4:1)

Jonah wanted God to carry out His threat of destruction because it would confirm him in his role and make him believable, but God was more concerned about the lost than about the prophet's reputation! Jonah forgot that the heart of God is always to forgive rather than judge. I have been in churches where prophecies exposed sexual sin or bad habits. When people responded they were lambasted with judging words instead of Jesus' grace and forgiveness. Marilyn once prayed with a young man struggling against homosexual tendencies who several times had publicly repented. Each time the churches focused on the awful nature of his sin, making him so condemned that he became completely withdrawn. He was talking with Marilyn about something else but she kept getting the word "homosexual". Eventually she asked him very gently if he had any problems of that nature. When he responded, she continued seeking the Lord and a long buried emotional hurt to do with his mother was revealed. At the end, although he still had a lot to work through, he knew that the Lord had met with him and loved him and was giving him the power to change.

A Prayer

"Lord Jesus, thank You that You only ever speak or act out of love. Please give me eyes to see as You see, ears to hear as You hear, a mouth to speak as You speak and a heart to love as You love. Amen."

CHAPTER 4

UNWRAPPING
HIS GIFTS

"When he, the Spirit of truth, comes, he will guide you into all
truth. He will not speak on his own; he will speak only what
he hears, and he will tell you what is yet to come.
He will bring glory to me by taking from what is mine
and making it known to you."
(JOHN 16:13–14)

I have been emphasizing that we need to ask God for
appropriate revelation and power to meet a need. However,
it is also vital we realise that God will initiate speaking to
us. In Samuel 3:1–14 we see how God calls Samuel's name

three times. Samuel was only a child and had never experienced hearing God's voice, nor was the culture at that time open to revelation from God. God broke into that lack of experience and expectation by taking the initiative, calling Samuel by name and then opening his ears to the prophetic. We see this happening again and again in the Bible, with many a prophet's account beginning: *"The word of the LORD came to me..."* This may happen in all kinds of ways: we may find a person is constantly on our minds. Maybe God wants us to pray for them or reach out in some way. We may have a phrase or visual impression or Bible verse come unexpectedly into our minds. We may suddenly be aware that something is not right, or have a feeling of urgency that we should do something.

Whatever the form is, the fact is, God is trying to get our attention and like Samuel we need to respond:

"Speak, for your servant is listening."

(1 SAMUEL 3:10)

I was once in an Anglican church which had an extremely high ceiling and I thought, you could fit another building up there and this church would still be tall! Suddenly, I "saw" another floor coming into place. It started at the very front of the building and slowly moved backwards until there was an entire new lower ceiling. Then I felt strongly that I should read Isaiah 58. This chapter calls God's people to serve those in need, feed the hungry, clothe the naked. I believed God wanted them to build an extra floor in the church to provide practical help for those in need. This was a very directive prophecy and I was reluctant to share it.

After all, if they acted on it and it was wrong it could cost them thousands! After I prayed however, I had a deep sense of peace that I should share it.

Later, I was amazed to hear that God had recently spoken to them in exactly the same way. They had begun to make enquiries to see how feasible it would be to have another floor put in and in doing so had discovered that the church was structurally unsound. A new church was going to be built and at the time I prophesied, they had been seeking for confirmation that they should still pursue the original vision!

FREE GIFTS FOR ALL!

Many people say to me, "I wish I could hear God like that!" Their unspoken meaning is that they feel unworthy and wrongly believe it is only the "special, spiritual" people who will be used in that way. This attitude is actually based on the Old Covenant where God would call a special individual to be His mouthpiece to the nation. While there were groups of prophets working together, they were still classed as a unique group and the ordinary Jew would not expect to prophesy.

A NEW DAY

Under the New Covenant, this all changed. The Old Testament prophets pointed to the coming Messiah and the Kingdom of God. Jesus' arrival fulfilled those prophecies (see Luke 4:17–21) and ushered in that Kingdom, giving the Holy Spirit to all believers. Rather than one special person prophesying, these are the days when we can *all* move in these gifts, because their purpose is now to establish and build the Kingdom of God and to see fulfilled the overthrow of Satan's kingdom. As Joel prophesied:

"I will pour out my Spirit on all people.
Your sons and daughters will prophesy,
   your old men will dream dreams,
   your young men will see visions.
Even on my servants, both men and women,
   I will pour out my Spirit in those days."

(JOEL 2:28–29)

By specifically referring to the fringe people groups – young, old, women, servants, Joel turned the traditional understanding of the one person prophet on its head. It is not simply that more people will be prophesying, but that the weak, previously disregarded members will be equally valuable and equally able to minister.

THE POWER OF A VISION FROM GOD

Joel refers to dreams and visions. What are these and how can God speak through something as vague as a dream?

Both dreams and visions are God-given pictures or ideas that impress themselves upon the inner mind's eye. The main difference between them is that you generally have a vision when you are awake and completely aware of all that is going on, but a dream usually occurs when you are asleep. The pictures conveyed in the dream/vision are given to bring godly challenge, new perception, healing, strategy for prayer and action or new vision and understanding of the glory of God. It is like a vivid scene or visual idea that comes into the mind. It can be frozen like a video on pause, or it can be moving like a video on play. It can be something completely innocuous like a doll or a bird, or something we may have had no actual experience of, like Ezekiel's visions of terrifying creatures with living wheels and eyes. However it comes and whatever it is, the vision originates with God and is communicated to us by the Holy Spirit. While it can be sparked off by something we see or experience, we do not manufacture it in our minds. It is more that God draws our attention to something. Once we have "seen" it, we can then ask God in "listening conversation" what it means and how He wants us to apply it. That stage is often neglected but is always vital. However experienced we are in hearing God, we can never presume that we know what God is saying. Often we will be taken by surprise as this following example illustrates.

I had a vision of someone walking along a street lined by tall imposing buildings. As they passed under a particular building I realised it was about to collapse. I tried to shout a warning but the person did not hear and continued walking. The next moment the building fell, burying them in the rubble.

This was horrific and yet I also had an overwhelming sense of God's healing love. I believed it symbolised achievements that the person had spent many years building up, but God had been pushed to the sidelines. In order to be truly strong and fulfilled they needed to bring Him back into their life's centre, otherwise those very achievements might collapse on top of them.

I shared the vision in this way and a lady on crutches responded. I asked her if she knew what the building represented and she told me some things that she realised she'd been giving too much time to. I was about to pray when she said,

"A building fell on me a few months ago, could that be relevant?"

I was stunned! "What do you mean?" I asked, taking her hand as tears filled her eyes.

"My husband and I were abroad on holiday," she swallowed. "It happened just like you described. We were shopping one day. It was a busy street, big buildings, crowds. We heard shouts but there was so much noise, we didn't think it was anything to do with us." She shook her head, her face white. "There was a terrible roar and shaking and then everything went black. I woke up in hospital with both legs injured. The building had been unsafe and just collapsed suddenly. Ten people were killed, my husband was one of them." She put her face in her hands and wept. "I feel so guilty that it was him and not me."

To say I was shocked was an understatement. I had been so sure that the vision was symbolic. I hadn't even asked the Lord if it was a real event because it just seemed so unlikely. Yet as Marilyn and I prayed for her to be healed of her trauma and guilt, I realised why I'd felt such an overwhelming sense of God's compassion. He cared so much about her accident and loss and that she was still plagued by terrifying flashbacks. With the vision she realised that God knew every detail and had even been there protecting her. She was able to let go of her guilt at being alive, release her husband to God and start to seek

Him for His plan for her life. She left that conference a different woman.

WHAT WAS HAPPENING?

Through this vision God was revealing specific knowledge of a past traumatic event in order to bring healing into her memories. The vision was like a video of something real that had happened. However, many visions are symbolic. By this, I mean that their purpose is to shine God's light into a true situation by use of an illustrative visual dynamic. Thus we see in Acts 10 the vision that God gave Peter when he was praying on the roof.

> *"He saw heaven opened and something like a large sheet being let down to earth by its four corners. It contained all kinds of four-footed animals, as well as reptiles of the earth and birds of the air. Then a voice told him, 'Get up, Peter. Kill and eat.'"*

(ACTS 10:11–13)

Unlike my vision of the falling building, this was not an action replay. No sheets full of animals had fallen from heaven! Instead, God was giving Peter a symbolic visual dynamic to challenge and change his cultural mindset. Peter's mind was closed to the idea of the Gentiles receiving God's grace, but there were Gentiles who wanted to become Christians on their way to his house at that very moment, sent by God's Spirit. The vision was like a cultural slap in the face! It caught Peter's attention and as he prayed and asked God what it meant he was given the specific interpretation and application. This prepared him in a dynamic way for their arrival and there was immediate powerful fruit as he led their entire household to salvation.

How Do I Get Revelation?

In the above example from Acts there were two dynamics at work. Firstly, the vision was entirely God-given. In other words, it did not originate through something that Peter saw that God then spoke through. Instead it was divinely inserted by the Holy Spirit into Peter's consciousness. This happened three times to enable Peter to grasp that this was truly a communication from God and not a flight of his imagination. However, although its origin was God-inspired, two things in Peter's life at that time acted as a magnet to the Holy Spirit. Look at these verses from Acts 10:

> *"About noon the following day ... Peter went up on the roof to pray. He became hungry and wanted something to eat, and while the meal was being prepared, he fell into a trance. He saw heaven opened..."*

(ACTS 10:9–11)

▶ *The trigger*

Although the vision is divinely created, there is still a human trigger – Peter's hunger! God used Peter's rumbling tummy as the trigger for the powerful vision! We can often push away our ordinary human needs, thinking, I'm so un-spiritual, but God made us with those needs! As we open up and welcome Him into the centre of our every day, those very needs can become triggers for His voice. Thus, in John

4:4–19 we see how Jesus is tired and thirsty as He sits by a well. It is His thirst that acts as the trigger for the Holy Spirit to speak into His mind about the approaching woman and *her* deep inner thirst. As He follows this impression and talks to the Spirit, He receives more divinely inspired knowledge about her five husbands and her current desperate lifestyle.

▶ *Prayer*

Peter had made a choice – to pray, to give time to be with God and hear His voice. Jesus constantly made the same choice. In the midst of crowds and pressures Jesus would create time to be with His Father, to talk with Him and discover His strategy for that moment. Jesus received all His power and anointing as He constantly engaged with the Holy Spirit in prayer. Now Peter was doing the same thing. Prayer was his priority even though he was hungry. He still continued to pray and seek God while the food was being prepared.

The fact is, prayer opens up our spirits to hear what God wants to tell us. It is *not* that by praying we are telling God: "See I'm praying, so You must give me a word now!" *Gifts are gifts not wages!* But as we pray, our focus tunes into God, our own agendas are put aside and He sees that we are open to Him and wanting His will. As a loving Father, not just to us, but to His world, He responds.

In my church once, the pastor's wife, Rachel, spoke to my friend Debbie, whereupon Debbie burst into tears and hugged her! It turned out that Debbie had been unwell all week with a bad ear infection. No antibiotics were working and she felt very low. Rachel did not know this, but she *was* praying for the church when Debbie came to her mind together with an overwhelming sense of God's love for her. Throughout that week, Rachel interceded for Debbie till the burden lifted. When they compared notes Debbie realised it was from that time she began to feel better. She was so amazed and thankful at the way God had loved her through Rachel. But that all happened as Rachel made prayer a priority and thus opened her spirit up to God's inspiration.

ORDINARY THINGS CAN CARRY PROPHETIC WEIGHT

During the ministry time in a conference, a lady carrying two heavy bags put them down and then came for some prayer. Suddenly I sensed that simple action had prophetic meaning. I told her that God wanted her to lay down some things in her life that were making her too busy. I was startled when she burst into tears. She had been feeling overstretched but had not known how to say no to demands. She was amazed how God had spoken in this way. The word from God showed her that He knew all about her struggle in this area and gave her the necessary impetus to change.

WHAT WAS HAPPENING?

My physically seeing the lady's action sparked off an awareness of her busyness. This was God-given knowledge that I had no way of knowing humanly. It was also prophetic in the sense that it revealed what God wanted to happen to help the lady develop a better lifestyle.

What the New Testament refers to as a "word" of knowledge is called such because it is usually only a single or small degree of information that we receive. In the above example, the knowledge came through observing a normal happening with God's illumination. Samuel had a similar thing happen to him as he discerned God's heart for King Saul through an actual physical thing he saw Saul do. The context is when Samuel tells Saul that because of disobedience, God has rejected him as king.

> *"Samuel said to him, 'I will not go back with you ... the LORD has rejected you as king over Israel!' As Samuel turned to leave, Saul caught hold of the hem of his robe, and it tore. Samuel said to him, 'The LORD has torn the kingdom of Israel from you today and has given it to one of your neighbours ...'"*
>
> (1 SAMUEL 15:26–28)

Saul's action of tearing the robe became, in that moment, a channel for God to speak through prophetically to Samuel. It wasn't that Samuel was rubbing Saul's nose in it, but the Holy Spirit was taking the simple action and speaking through it into Samuel's spirit.

GOD IS THERE AS A FRIEND

The way God spoke in these examples was unexpected and "unreligious". It was as if He was there as a friend (which of course He was!), breaking into our thoughts by pointing His finger at something real and tangible and saying, "Look at that, see what that means!" and so giving powerful insight into each situation.

Similarly, you can know specifically what God is saying, but have no idea who the recipient may be. One of our prayer team, Lilian, was enjoying watching some ducks at a conference centre, but suddenly realised that God was speaking to her prophetically through them. Over several days she received some beautiful messages from Father God to His beloved child all springing from her Spirit-illumined observation of the ducks. She shared these messages in the meetings and many were blessed.

GOD SEES
THE FULL PURPOSE

Revelation can come from something you've seen, but you can also suddenly "know", as if a phrase, impression, picture or an idea about someone or about a situation has just dropped into your consciousness.

Sometimes a simple piece of knowledge is all you get and you don't know what God wants to do. It is very tempting to presume that you know and rush in with your prayers or advice. But God always shows things for a purpose and it's not always what we expect! The other day, I had two phrases come to my mind: "gynaecological problems" and "sinus problems". That was all I knew and all I shared. At the end, two sisters came up who had those conditions but who also had very deep emotional pain. The physical problems were "safe" enough for them to feel they could respond, but during prayer it was the much deeper pain that God brought to the surface and started to touch.

The Key to Accurately Receiving and Interpreting Revelation Is Conversing with God

In Peter's roof experience, Peter did not only receive the vision, he conversed about it with God. The sheet of unclean animals was let down:

> *"Then a voice told him, 'Get up, Peter. Kill and eat.'*
> *'Surely not, Lord!' Peter replied. 'I have never eaten anything impure or unclean.'*
> *The voice spoke to him a second time, 'Do not call anything impure that God has made clean.'*
> *This happened three times . . . "*

(Acts 10:13–16)

The vision on its own had no meaning other than to repulse. God then initiated a conversation about it and Peter heard Him and answered from his human and cultural standpoint. God then took Peter's words and spoke again giving Peter further understanding of what the vision might mean. Three times God went over this. He is always patient and will keep reinforcing His message to us. We need to ensure that we give God time to reveal the meaning to us by questioning and conversing with Him, checking it is rooted in Scripture and that our hearts are right and full of God-given peace before we share or act. Satan will try to deceive us, as will our own heart, but as we humbly keep seeking to love God more fully and know Him in Scripture, we will grow in our ability to discern what is truly from Him and what is from the devil or our own imagination.

PROPHECY

The Good News Bible describes prophecy as speaking out God's message. It is often actual words and phrases that we "hear" in our minds and speak out as from God. It is not infallible like the Scriptures and must always be weighed by their authority. It is an incredibly powerful and decisive tool to transform individuals and situations.

The message itself can take all sorts of forms and can be given by God for all sorts of reasons. He may want to speak tender words of comfort and peace. As Paul says:

"Everyone who prophesies speaks to men for their strengthening, encouragement and comfort."

(1 CORINTHIANS 14:3)

I was praying with someone recently who was very ill. My inclination was to focus on the illness and pray for God's healing and strength to flow into her body. However, I found myself speaking prophetic words of love to her as if she was an abandoned and fearful child. The prophecy had almost the feel of a lullaby, rich in God's tender Father love. It then looked to the future with the same tender assurance that she was eternally held in His love and He could never abandon her. She wept as I spoke this over her and later wrote to say that the grief of her childhood was now much more healed.

On the other hand God may want to challenge an individual, family, church, community or even a nation through a prophetic word. This type of prophecy will often have a strong element of "seeing" beyond the outward appearance of a situation to the hidden reality and from there looking to the future and what God wants to do. John's prophetic words to the seven churches in Revelation are like this.

Graham Cooke, the well known prophetic minister is passionate about hearing the voice of God. Through diligent and humble practice he has developed a spiritual ear that is truly in tune with God's voice. As he listens to the Holy Spirit in all kinds of situations, God reveals specific knowledge of people's needs. But Graham never stops just there. He continues to ask God for more understanding as to what the revelation might mean and for wisdom to know how to apply it. Here is one of the stories from his book, *Developing Your Prophetic Gifting*:

"Prophecy can reveal to people exactly what is on God's heart now and what we should do next in response to the moving of the Spirit ... The Lord showed me that there was a woman who had been fasting and praying for her wayward daughter. He showed me that this mother was desperately concerned that her rebellious daughter would get into drug related problems or be taken advantage of sexually ... The prophetic word told the mother that God had heard her prayers and was moving to answer them ... The mother was to cease praying and begin giving thanks and praising God for His involvement. For several months afterwards the mother gave thanks and praised God. In the early period very little changed ... The mother held on to the prophetic word and continued in praise and gratitude to the Lord. Not only has her daughter been fully restored to the Lord and her mother, but the woman's life has been changed immeasurably. She now has a spirit of thanksgiving and a grateful heart." [5]

An Exercise

1. Spend time worshipping and enjoying God's presence.
2. Think of a person, situation or an upcoming church meeting where you would love to see the Lord's power at work. Pray about it and ask Jesus what is needed to release His blessing.
3. Listen with your spiritual ears for any "words" or feelings that come to you, or you may find your attention drawn to a Bible verse or to something you are looking at or thinking about.
4. Talk to Him about any revelation and ask Him to give you more understanding and maybe scriptural confirmation. Ask Jesus to show you it is from Him by giving you inner peace.
5. If you think you should share it, ask for a gift of wisdom to know how and when to share.
6. When you do share, ask Jesus to cover your words and manner with His love. Speak sensitively and leave them room to respond in their own way.
7. Keep listening even while you share as He may give you more revelation or show you how to pray for them.
8. Go for it! If God has entrusted us with something precious we need to obey Him and step out.

CHAPTER 5

GROWING AND MATURING

"Speaking the truth in love, we will in all things grow up into him who is the Head, that is, Christ. From him the whole body, joined and held together by every supporting ligament, grows and builds itself up in love, as each part does its work."

(EPHESIANS 4:15–16)

WHAT'S HAPPENING IN MY HEART?

There is a lifetime of steps and experiences between learning about the spiritual gifts, stepping out in those gifts, and becoming "a prophet" or "a healer". But one realisation is vital: all who want the gifts are actually seeking to minister the heart and love of God.

The Corinthians went wrong because they saw having the gifts as a mark of spiritual superiority. They were crowing over one another and competing instead of using the gifts in a united spirit of service to the Church and community. We may think, "I could never do that", but we all do it, even the disciples had to be corrected by Jesus. The evidence of power so easily goes to our heads. The key is to keep our focus on the greatness of God. A man in my church once shared about someone looking for a lady who was known as "the mighty woman of God". When they eventually found her, she said "Oh, you've got it wrong – I'm the little woman of a Mighty God." That attitude is the hallmark of true growth and maturity.

Oh Dear!

Once I became intoxicated with the idea of being known as "a prophet"! I knew people were awed by anything specific so decided that was how God was anointing me as it would bring such glory to His name! In front of a crowd I picked out a young girl and stated:

"Your name is Pauline isn't it?"

She looked confused. "No," she said, "my name is Dawn."

Unfortunately, to me, "Dawn" sounds very like "Pauline" and I thought she had agreed! I preened myself, saying, "God told me your name because He loves you and wants you to know that He sees the struggle you are having at college and is going to help you."

She looked even more confused. "But I'm not at college," she said. "I work in a shop and enjoy it!"

I heard this bit and was taken aback, but quickly came in again. "Oh, maybe I got that a touch wrong, Pauline," I said, patting her on the shoulder. "I believe God is saying to not get too settled in your shop but to trust Him to take the step to go to college!"

Mercifully, at this point someone slipped a note in my hand saying, "Tracy, her name is Dawn *not* Pauline, and she is thrilled about her job in the shop. God led her there after ages of her trying to find jobs. Maybe you'd better listen to God again!" I apologised and beat a hasty retreat! I was sure I had forfeited my genuine prophetic gifting, but God is so merciful. He just wanted me to make a bit of a fool of myself so that I could get my motives right! Me looking good as a prophet carried no weight with Him! Rather, He wanted a "me" who was willing to love as He loves.

MISTAKES, CURSE OR BLESSING?

We all dread making a mistake. Many of us refrain from stepping out altogether because we feel so afraid we'll get it wrong. On the other hand, we can become so self-confident that we give up checking our revelations against God's Word or asking Him for more clarification. But the key to our growth and maturity is realising that we *are* easily deceived and yet, incredibly, God still uses us.

A baby learning to walk makes mistakes all the time and learns from them! In listening to God we are like babies, always learning, always experimenting, always making mistakes and learning again and thus, step by step, growing up and becoming more like Jesus. The aim of our growth is not that people see us as polished and successful in all we do, after all, it would be us that got the glory then! But that they see Jesus who *"... chose the weak things of this world to shame the strong"* (1 Corinthians 1:27).

God simply wants us to be open to His voice and willing to step out even if we don't always understand why.

We see in Acts how Ananias needed to forfeit his lack of understanding when God asked him to go to Saul's accommodation and pray for his healing.

"Ananias answered, 'I have heard many reports about this man and all the harm he has done ... he has come here with authority from the chief priests to arrest all who call on your name.'

But the Lord said to Ananias, 'Go! This man is my chosen instrument...'

Then Ananias went..."

(ACTS 9:13–15, 17)

Everything in Ananias' mind told him this was mad. He could be killed for doing such a thing! God did not pamper to his fear but asked him to step out in trust and obedience. How wonderful that he was willing to do that even though it might be a terrible mistake.

OUR NEED FOR WISDOM

"If any of you lacks wisdom, he should ask God, who gives generously to all without finding fault, and it will be given to him."

(JAMES 1:5)

Do we come to our Father God with a joyful expectation that He will willingly give us all the wisdom we need? The Book of Proverbs makes it clear that Jesus Himself is our Wisdom, so when we ask Father God for wisdom we are actually asking for some time with our beloved Jesus.

Jesus Himself was the supreme example of our need to keep opening up to God for more understanding. He said in John 8:28, *"I do nothing on my own but speak just what the Father has taught me."* He constantly sought for guidance as to how to answer people and know how to minister. He was able to declare with assurance that He could say and do nothing other than what He saw His Father doing. This is the essence of our own journey to grow and mature, that we might know God and be part of what He is doing.

Too Quick to Share

I realised my own need to constantly come to God for wisdom in a terrible situation I created one day in my impetuosity to share a word.

During a concert I had a growing sense that God wanted to speak encouragement to a woman who was having trouble conceiving. As I prayed about this I seemed to suddenly "see" that the problem had its roots in something her mother had done to her before she was even born. I felt excited by this, thinking that it could be a real breakthrough for the woman. If she could be emotionally healed then maybe she would have her baby. Without stopping to think, I jumped to my feet and shared this "word" exactly as it came to me.

Afterwards a group of ladies came up looking distressed. "We think your word was for our friend. She hasn't been able to conceive but she'd never had any idea her mother might have done such a thing to her. She's gone home very upset. What shall we do?"

I was stunned! Not until that moment had I realised how devastating such a word could be, not just for the person it was intended for, but for everyone there having trouble conceiving. The nature of the word was such that there was no way the person could check it out and so put her heart at rest. Unless the Lord gave her supernatural peace she could be forever suspecting her mother.

That night the Lord spoke into my heart:

"Why didn't you wait until you knew what I wanted you to do? Why didn't you check it out with Me and seek My wisdom first? Why did you put giving a word before giving My love?"

Two days later I received a letter from the pastor saying that he was concerned by the word and the number of people that had been upset. He pointed out that as the church was just beginning to move out into the spiritual gifts, many people had been frightened away.

Grieved, I wrote to the pastor, confessing I had been wrong to bring the word and asking him to pass on to the people concerned how very sorry I was to have caused such hurt. The pastor wrote back very lovingly, forgiving and releasing me from the guilt of what had happened. He also expressed his continued support for us, which deeply touched me.

An Exercise

Make some time to be quiet with the Lord and ask Him to come and speak to you by His Spirit. Ponder these verses:

> *"The unfailing love of the LORD never ends ... Great is his faithfulness; his mercies begin afresh each day. I say to myself, 'The LORD is my inheritance; therefore, I will hope in him!'"*
> (LAMENTATIONS 3:22–24 NLT)

Ask the Holy Spirit, who is both the Convictor and Comforter, to remind you of the last time you feel you messed up with God. For example, when you didn't listen to Him properly, held back from speaking out, said the wrong thing, failed to change after He'd spoken to you about an area of your life etc.

1. In the light of these verses how are you viewing that messed up time?
2. Are you at peace that it is covered by the "unfailing love" of your Lord and blotted out by His mercies?
3. Or are you still focused on what went wrong?
4. Have you made any negative choices in the light of what happened? e.g. "I will never try that again!"
5. What does it mean to you that His mercies are fresh every day?
6. In the light of that fact, are you willing to give both what went wrong and your resulting negative choices to Jesus and thank Him for His fresh love and mercies?
7. Do you really see the Lord as being your inheritance or are you deep down looking to success and applause as your reward? If you become aware this is the case (and it

is to some degree in all of us), don't be condemned! Simply tell the Lord about it and ask Him to release you and centre you completely on Him.

8. Spend some time thankfully worshipping Him and listening to Him. Ask Him to fill you with new strength and resources.

COMMUNITY AWARENESS

Although the way we hear God is always individual, the outworking of it is always communal. Even a completely personal word from God will bear communal fruit. Think of Gideon. When he was in a place of extreme weakness, God spoke to him through an angel, saying,

> *"The LORD is with you, mighty warrior."*
>
> (JUDGES 6:12)

The fact that God gave him a name that was so opposite to the truth, opened Gideon's heart for him to be released of his fear and become the man God had made him to be, in very fact, Mighty Warrior. But although this was personal to Gideon, its effect was immediately felt in the community. The nation moved from a place of slavery and oppression to freedom and victory all because God spoke and continued to speak to one man.

Similarly, when Jesus spoke to the woman at the well (John 4), He was speaking to her personally and privately, revealing His knowledge of her inner thirst and sinful lifestyle. She took into her heart the fact that His words were from God and there was an immediate communal effect:

"The woman went back to the town and said to the people, 'Come, see a man who told me everything I ever did. Could this be the Christ?' They came out of the town and made their way towards him ... Many of the Samaritans from that town believed in him because of the woman's testimony..."

(JOHN 4:28–30, 39)

WATCH FOR OUR BAD FRUIT

The above examples underline the positive and sometimes dramatically powerful effects on others as we seek to hear God's voice. However, as stated earlier, it is vital that we seek to grow and mature primarily in our innermost beings, as it is from here that God works most powerfully to reveal His love through our lives. But it is also from here that our un-dealt-with insecurities and reactions to hurts can cause a very negative communal effect. The following story illustrates this:

> "Do you mind if I have a chat?" The woman standing over me introduced herself and sat down.
>
> "Sharon," she started forcefully, "I have some strong words for you from the Lord."
>
> "Really?" The guards I keep around my tender heart went back up!
>
> "Sharon, I just know I have to say something. Well, it's like this. I was praying about you and your relationship with Hugo and the Lord showed me that you are proud!"
>
> How kind of Him, I thought, wondering what was still to come.

"You have pride in your heart. It is pride in your ability to be free to minister, preach and travel. You are holding onto this against God's will. You need to let it go! You need to give your husband Hugo what he really wants in life, and stop denying him!"

There was a pause for breath, then a long stare. She was trying to read my face.

"So what am I denying Hugo?" I asked wearily, knowing what was probably coming.

"Children! He wants family! And your pride and desire for a ministry career is stopping him!" She smiled with triumph. She had said what she came to say. Got it out of her system. Given God's Word!?

What could I say to the poor lady? She was obviously very upset about something. This was her way to cope with it. I had to be nice and kind. But inside I wanted to thump her!

I had two objections. Firstly, *I am medically infertile.*

Secondly, she wanted to have a go at me and she was using a pretence at prophecy to remove herself from having to take responsibility for her words . . . [6]

In this situation, as Sharon discerned, the woman had an un-dealt-with wound in her life that she was allowing to masquerade as prophecy. She wouldn't have seen it as that. She was hearing a voice that she believed was righteous judgement. Ironically, she was accusing Sharon of pride, but it was her own pride that was blinding her to the fact that she was speaking out of the desire to control rather than the desire to love.

There can be a subtle attraction in giving words of

knowledge and prophecy. To know something that no one else knows, to have the power to be "God" to the "lesser" people around you who aren't so spiritual as you!

WE MUST BE MOTIVATED BY LOVE

Each time I hear of such stories or fall into the same trap myself, I feel saddened that such a beautiful gift from God can be so misused. Often there is a genuine desire to encourage someone, but interpreting these desires alone as the definite word of God, creates a false spiritual authority that can have devastating results. God's thoughts and ways are so much higher than our own and our own hearts can deceive us. We may think we know God's very best for someone and pray/prophesy accordingly, but it must be God's all-seeing, all-powerful love that fills, controls and speaks through us. As Paul says:

> *"If I speak in the tongues of men and of angels, but have not love, I am only a resounding gong or a clanging symbol. If I have the gift of prophecy and can fathom all mysteries and all knowledge, and if I have a faith that can move mountains, but have not love, I am nothing."*
>
> (1 CORINTHIANS 13:1–2)

DELIVERING PROPHECY

In the above example the lady delivered her "word" in a very intimidating way. It put Sharon in a corner and gave her no room to respond or escape. From the way many of us give words, you might think that God is some kind of sergeant major, instead of the one who is *"full of grace and truth"* (John 1:14).

What really is being conveyed when we share a word in a "listen or else", kind of way? We may think, "Well, God has shown me their sin and I mustn't undermine His message by being wishy-washy!" But what we're really conveying is our own arrogant self-righteousness rather than God's mercy and grace. Have we really taken time to study how Jesus spoke to people? Look at how He handled the paralysed man (Mark 2:1–12). He didn't thump the man over the head with His Spirit-inspired knowledge of the man's sin. He simply said, *"Son, your sins are forgiven!"* (v. 5).

Rather than use the Bible to build the fruit and character of Jesus in our lives so that we minister like Him, many of us think that God has to use our favourite translation and speak His messages in sixteenth-century English! Can you imagine Jesus ranting on with a fifteen minute prophecy full of "Thee's", "Thou's" and "Thus saith the Lord's"?!

I've fallen into the trap of giving long wordy prophecies many times and on occasion have put people in a corner too. But I am trying more and more to trust God with the outcome of the word and deliver it sensitively. Rather than saying definitely, "God says this…!" I now say, "I had the impression that … could this be true?" I then listen for the person's response while still listening to God in my heart and take it from there.

GETTING THE BALANCE

We meet people who refuse to believe that God will speak in any other way than what He has already made known through the Bible and others who talk at length about the constant new words and pictures God has given them.

It is when we base everything on what we feel God has shown us, that we make mistakes. I sometimes feel, "Goodness these people are so spiritual, I could never hear God like that!" But when we question some of them more closely, we see that they are relying on their revelations more than the Bible and sometimes even abandoning the Bible altogether! We may think, "What does that matter? I know the Bible so well already, what's important now is to have a real, present communication with God."

JESUS SHOWS US THE WAY

When Jesus was attacked in the wilderness it was with that same subtle temptation, to follow His own desires, to doubt the Word of God and to make God's Word say something it doesn't. Jesus did not discuss these issues with Satan, or try to rationalise how they could be right for Him. He just answered each statement with the simple words, "It is written..." God's Word was His foundation stone and nothing could make Him swerve from it. From that point it says that the Holy Spirit came upon Him in power and He was launched into His ministry of signs and wonders, with divine authority and incredible love and compassion.

A PRAYER

"Lord Jesus, thank You that love for Your Father was what constantly motivated You. You loved and knew the Word of

God and it was the foundation of all You thought, said and did. You listened ceaselessly to Your Father and carried out His strategies.

Lord You know that I make many mistakes and am often led by my insecurities and desires rather than by Your Holy Spirit. Please forgive me. Please take my mistakes and use them to help me grow more like You, overflowing with Your love and compassion. Please set my feet on the foundation of Your Word and give me such a longing for Your truth that the devil will not be able to make me swerve from it. Please fill me with Your wonderful Spirit and release Your gifts within me, enabling me to hear Your voice and know Your heart. Thank You, Jesus. Amen."

AM I BEING A GOOD "BODY PART"?

Remember that primarily we are seeking to build up the Body of Christ through our gifting. As Paul said, *"Now to each one the manifestation of the Spirit is given for the **common good"** (1 Corinthians 12:7, emphasis added).

Part of that building up is achieved through the way we regard our leaders and those around us. Paul says, *"Honour one another above yourselves"* (Romans 12:10). However right we feel a word is, on occasion we will need to be willing to let it go if a leader feels it should not be shared or even if they forget it! Our responsibility is to offer it and then trust Him with the outcome.

Paul teaches us the strategies we should follow to administer directive prophecy safely so that God is truly glorified:

"Two or three prophets should speak, and the others should weigh carefully what is said."

(1 CORINTHIANS 14:29)

This is about the need to make ourselves accountable. However experienced and accurate we are in listening to God, we will always be fallible. I tell someone else, usually Marilyn, or the leader of a church, before I share anything that is very directional. Many times Marilyn has enabled me to see the need for caution in how I share something, whereas I am often too caught up in it to take that kind of objective stand. If a leader feels that it is from God it gives me extra confidence to share it with God's authority.

WORKING TOGETHER

I am often aware of a jealous, competitive element in me and other prophetic people. If one person is asked to share a word, then I feel I must give one too! If I don't receive the same attention as another prophet, I can feel rejected! But these feelings are in direct contrast to the whole reason for which they are given. Rather than feeling threatened when confronted with other prophets, we need to be honouring and praying for them. Where there is a genuine openness to the Lord and love for one another a beautiful harmony occurs. What one prophet shares will often correlate with another in a way that makes you know "God has truly spoken". We had this happen in a small group once when we were praying for a man who was struggling spiritually. We quietly listened to God, praying that He would lead us and bless this person, then we shared together and it was incredible – a picture, a verse, an encouraging thought, an insight into a past memory – as each person shared there was such a sense of the presence of God. The man was bowled over, knowing as never before that God both knew and loved him.

A FINAL EXERCISE!

1. Get together with a small group (3 or 4), all of you wanting to bless others and hear God's voice.
2. Spend time worshipping together.
3. Choose one of the group to be blessed in prayer. The rest quietly pray and listen to the Lord for that person. Ask Him how He wants to bless or affirm them. Take note of anything that comes and keep praying for them.
4. After an appropriate time, each share with the person, taking care to be sensitive.
5. Ask if they want to respond and then cement what has been shared with prayer.
6. Do the same for each member of the group.

Conclusion

A Meditation

Peter was in a hurry. He needed to get to the temple and time was running out. The crowds were as dense as always and the gate as narrow. He kept his eyes on the way ahead, blind to those jostling on either side of him. He had to be at the temple on time.

The crippled man was tired. Tired of sitting at this gate, tired of the hard, dusty roadside, the hordes of people, the ceaseless aching in his shattered legs. He felt invisible, unwanted. No one even looked at him, they just dropped their coins at his feet and walked on, their duty done. And that was if they gave at all! Many were the days he got nothing. Did they think he wanted to live like this, without any hope or pride? How did they think it felt to be picked up, carried and dumped again just like so much rubbish?

Another crowd. Wearily, he accosted them, crying his whine for help with practised ease. No one looked at him. Just the occasional patter of their smallest coins in his outstretched hand. Sometimes he felt more hungry for human contact than he did even for food.

Two men were upon him now. He recognised them. They'd come with *that* man, Jesus, who was supposed to do great things, even heal people born blind. Well, he'd been born crippled but nothing of that had come *his* way, even though Jesus had passed right by ... He *had* looked though. At least twice Jesus looked him right in the eye and each time he'd felt a strange warmth touching him inside. Well, no harm trying the friends ...

Peter stopped. Something was pulling at him. A man's hand, a beggar tugging at his robe. A cry for help, for money. Well, Peter had none. He wasn't earning any more so what could he be expected to give? Besides, he had to get to the temple. But Peter could not move. People were crowding him, cross, impatient. But there was something, some voice, the voice he loved, calling, insisting. Peter turned to the man. "Look at me," he said.

Shock surged through the man. He had actually been seen, heard. For once he would truly receive. He gladly looked at Peter, but no coins fell and in the confused pause his hand dropped back to his side.

Peter gazed into the beggar's face and a stillness came over him. Deep within he heard the voice he loved: "You've got Me, Peter. Give him Me, help him walk to Me." For a moment he hesitated, aware again of the thrusting crowds, the sheer impossibility of this man walking. But he knew what he'd heard and this time he was going to follow that voice and nothing else. He smiled into the beggar's hard, blank eyes and reached to grasp his hand.

"I don't have any money, but I give you what I do have ..." He pulled gently, sensing the Holy Spirit's power even as he spoke. "In the name of Jesus Christ of Nazareth, walk!" The impossible happened. Before his eyes those twisted legs uncurled, grew, straightened. The man rose up, crying out in incredulous joy. Feeling and strength born in place of death. Leaping, running, praising God.

(see Acts 3:1–31)

LETTING GOD SPEAK THROUGH YOU

What an awesome story of how God can speak and act through us to restore lives. Yet what a different story this would have been if Peter had not chosen to stop, listen and then act on what God showed him. His words to the beggar displayed the incredible power that is released when we let God speak through us. But Peter had to be willing to step out and be vulnerable. He'd already made so many public mistakes. It would have been much easier just to pass by. After all, no one would know what God had just told him to do.

But Peter refused to let his past negatively control his present. But it *did* control his present in that he now wanted to take every possible opportunity to work together with Jesus. He had fully received Jesus' forgiveness for his mistakes. He knew and loved Jesus and this time he was going to follow His voice whatever the cost.

THE FRUIT

As we saw earlier, whenever we respond personally to the voice of God, there is always fruit. Fruit not just in our own growth, but in the powerful effects that ripple out into the community. This principle is shown dynamically in this story. Here is just a bare summary of the fruit of Peter's listening obedience:

- A man miraculously healed and made full of praise to God.
- Crowds praising God.
- Two dynamic opportunities to preach the gospel.
- Thousands becoming Christians.
- Religious leaders forced to acknowledge they had killed the Christ and were now powerless to stop Jesus working through His disciples.
- Peter anointed to preach with greater power and authority.
- All the believers made aware of their need of God and through their prayers empowered to speak boldly of Jesus.

Do you want this kind of fruit in your life? I know I do! Then let's, like Peter, be willing to stop, not just in church, but right where we are, whenever Jesus calls us. Let's be willing to listen to what He says, even when it means letting go of our own understanding or security. Let's be willing to step out and do what He asks us to do.

> **There's nothing more transforming than hearing God speak. There's nothing more humbling than Almighty God choosing to speak and act *through me and you*.**

It's my prayer that having read this book you'll be inspired and equipped to let God do just that.

NOTES

1. Originally in my first book *The Voice of the Father*, Hodder & Stoughton, 1996.
2. "When I think", © Marilyn Baker, from *Face to Face*, 1992, Word (UK).
3. This prophetic word of encouragement came to me as I was actually writing this chapter. It is for you!
4. "Rest In My Love", 1987 by Marilyn Baker. Now on *Changing Me/Overflow of Worship* © Springtide/Word Music UK (Copycare).
5. Graham Cooke, *Developing Your Prophetic Gifting*, © Sovereign World Ltd, 1994, 2003, p. 39.
6. Hugo & Sharon Anson, *Some Mothers Do Have 'em, Others Don't*, © 1997 H & S Anson, Eagle Publishing, p. 1.

READING LIST

For all interested in learning more about the gifts of the Spirit.

Mike Bickle, *Growing in the Prophetic*, ©1995, Kingsway.

Cindy Jacobs, *The Voice of God*, © 1995, Regal Books.

Graham Cooke, *Developing Your Prophetic Gifting*, © 1994, 2003, Sovereign World.

Jack Deere, *The Beginners Guide to Prophecy*, © 2001, Vine Books.

Sam Storms, *The Beginners Guide to Spiritual Gifts*, © 2002, Regal Books.

FOR INFORMATION

If you would like information about Tracy Williamson or Marilyn Baker Ministries, please contact:

Marilyn Baker Ministries
PO Box 393
Tonbridge
Kent
TN9 9AY

Tel: 08707 501720
Email: info@marilynbakerministries.org
Website: www.marilynbakerministries.org

About the Author

Tracy Williamson was born in 1964 in North East London. At the age of two she became ill with encephalitis, which left her deaf and partially sighted with coordination difficulties. The hearing loss was not discovered until Tracy was twelve, which meant that she was often thought to be a slow learner. When Tracy was seven her father died of cancer. Soon afterwards a new father came into the family. He turned out to be a violent tempered man which had a damaging effect throughout Tracy's teen years.

These childhood traumas had a huge negative impact on Tracy's life and she became very introverted and depressed. Despite that and her deafness, she pushed forward in her academic achievements, becoming a wide reader and gaining GCSE and A-Levels, excelling particularly in English. When she was eighteen she was offered a place at what is now Hertfordshire University to take a teaching degree in the hope of becoming a teacher of the deaf.

Tracy's first year at college was fraught as she came to realise that she couldn't simply leave her past behind. Also her deafness made the teaching of children too stressful.

After a long period of anguished soul searching Tracy made the decision to give up her dream of teaching the deaf and transferred to a BA Degree in English Literature and Education. This whole process made her desperate for real answers and help in her life and after many conversations with Christian students, she became a Christian in June 1983. Tracy then went on to complete her degree, gaining a 2.1 (Hons.) in June 1985.

MINISTRY

In that same year, prior to forging a career with the visually impaired, Tracy met with blind singer/songwriter Marilyn Baker and a deep bond of friendship formed between them. Marilyn's assistant left in January 1986 and Marilyn asked Tracy to help her out temporarily. It soon became apparent however, that God was calling Tracy to the ministry and she gave up her proposed course to become Marilyn's personal assistant in April 1986. She is still in this ministry today.

TRACY'S ROLE

Initially Tracy's main role was to be a practical support and administrative assistant to Marilyn. However, it soon became clear that God had anointed Tracy with gifts of communication. Beginning with sharing her testimony in concerts, Tracy then began to receive prophetic words for individuals and churches. As her prophetic gifting developed, Tracy realised how few people expected God to speak to them personally. This led to her volunteering to do a workshop on listening to God at a conference led by

Jennifer Rees-Larcombe in 1993. The workshop was a great success and ultimately led to the publication of her first book *The Voice of the Father* which was published by Hodder and Stoughton in 1996.

Since then Tracy has written a number of articles promoting Marilyn's albums for various Christian publications. She has also written for Scripture Union's Bible reading notes series *Closer to God*, including a series on "The Father Heart of God" in 2001 and on the book of 2 Timothy in 2004. Her first book in this series, *Expecting God to Speak to You!*, was released in 2005. Tracy now regularly teaches at workshops, church weekends and conferences that she and Marilyn lead together. Some of the areas she teaches on are: prophetic prayer and ministry; prophetic evangelism; intimacy with God; the Father heart of God; breaking out of loneliness; overcoming fear and anxiety, and becoming the true Body of Christ.

BY THE SAME AUTHOR

In her first book, the ideal companion to this book, Tracy Williamson helps us to learn to *tune in* to God's voice in a variety of circumstances and gives practical advice on how to hear God better. This book will revitalize your prayer life.

We hope you enjoyed reading this New Wine book.
For details of other New Wine books and
a range of 2,000 titles from other
Word and Spirit publishers visit our website:
www.newwineministries.co.uk